UP YOURS

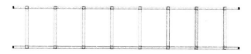

FINDING AND CLIMBING
YOUR LADDER OF SUCCESS

JOSH LISKE

emerge
publishing

TULSA, OKLAHOMA

19 18 17 16   10 9 8 7 6 5 4 3 2 1

UP YOURS
Finding and Climbing Your Ladder of Success

© 2016 Josh Liske

Published by:
Emerge Publishing, LLC
9521B Riverside Parkway, Suite 243
Tulsa, Oklahoma 74137
Phone: 888.407.4447
www.EmergePublishing.com

Cover Design: Christian Ophus | Emerge Publishing, LLC
Interior Design: Anita Stumbo

ISBN: 978-1-943127-22-1 Paperback
ISBN: 978-1-943127-19-1 Digital

Library of Congress Cataloging-in-Publication Data
BISAC Category:
BUS025000 BUSINESS & ECONOMICS / Entrepreneurship
BUS060000 BUSINESS & ECONOMICS / Small Business

Printed in the United States of America.

What People Are Saying

Josh Liske is an entrepreneur and business leader who talks his talk and walks his walk. If you are serious about climbing the ladder of success, Up Yours *will give you the principles and strategies to guarantee you reach the top. This book should be required reading for any aspiring business leader. If I had this book 20 years ago, I am certain I would have doubled my success. Don't just read this book, devour it!*

—MATT MORRIS, #1 Bestselling Author
The Unemployed Millionaire, www.MattMorris.com

Up Yours *is full of encouraging and timely advice making the book must read not only for those seeking business success but for anyone who desires to live a life grounded in integrity and faith.*

—PETER LISKE, proud father of Josh Liske
Captain of F/V Lady Alaska on TV show
Deadliest Catch, Season One, Discovery Channel

Up Yours *is an outstanding inspiration for success upon Josh Liske evidenced by The providential hand of God that activates prosperity and increase. It is a marketplace script of a leader whose journey up the ladder of triumph is a must read. The attributes of Purpose, Attitude and Faith enunciated for instance underscores the unfailing principles of a seasoned and a tested life.*

A ladder can either take you up or down but the choice of leaning on the everlasting Arms of The Lord with a consistent strong believe system is the assured reason for a never ending advancement upward to the top in all endeavors.

Josh (and Gina) carry along with them the ability to motivate teams, individuals and atmospheres wherever they go. May you take notes and enjoy Up Yours.

—DR. EMMANUEL ZIGA
President & Founder of Grace For All Nations,
Sr. Pastor of Sunshine Christian Church, www.GFANMI.org

The proven steps revealed in this book are innovative and will release you to new levels of success and fulfillment.

—DR. BOB HARRISON
America's Increase Authority, www.Increase.org

Did you know that 98% of people in the world will never live the life of their dreams simply because they don't know a few key strategies needed to leave the herd and join the achievers 2% club? Josh Liske gives you the secure steps on your ladder to achieving those things in life that others only envy. Up Yours is a great book that gives you the specific steps needed to transform your life or organization in order to go to the next level ... and beyond.

The last thing you want to do is work really hard your entire life to climb the ladder of success only to realize when you finally get to the top that you put your ladder on the wrong house. I know, I have tried in the past to climb my own ladder to the top without knowing these strategic steps and I failed miserably. Avoid the pain of making more mistakes and the negative feelings of being stuck by getting the wisdom contained in this great book by someone who is living his life in the top 2% club.

—DR. KEITH JOHNSON,
America's #1 Confidence Coach, www.KeithJohnson.TV

Watch your THOUGHTS,
they BECOME WORDS.

Watch your WORDS,
they BECOME ACTIONS.

Watch your ACTIONS,
they BECOME HABITS.

Watch your HABITS,
they BECOME CHARACTER.

Watch your CHARACTER,
for it BECOMES YOUR DESTINY.

—FRANK OUTLAW
Late President of the Bi-Lo Stores

CONTENTS

FOREWORD

AS HE ENTERED THE ROOM I immediately felt his grand presence. Not because he's a big man, but because of the attitude that followed his each and every step.

Standing in front of me was a man that had a purpose, a mission and a vision for what he was committed to achieving and I immediately knew that no matter what goals he set that day, he would achieve them.

If you've ever observed an eagle stare at it's prey, this was the focus that Josh had the entire day we were together planning one of his greatest business successes: *To become the #1 Franchise in his industry.*

As you read and absorb the wisdom in this book, you will find what all great students and highly successful people discover: *Success is achieved by setting a clear vision and then, being relentless everyday in your pursuit to achieving it.*

Success isn't about doing 100 things a few times. It's about doing the critical few things that really matter, hundreds of times instead of the trivial many things that don't really move the needle. In this book, you will find those critical few things and when you apply them, they will guarantee your success.

The simplicity of each success factor that you will learn, will make it easy for you to achieve exponential growth and personal success. How do I know this to be true? Because success leaves clues and what Josh practices and teaches has withstood the test of time and works for anyone who works them.

Many years ago after setting some big goals for my life, my mentor asked me if I was interested or if I was committed to achieving my life's goals and dreams and then he said: *"If you are interested you will come up with stories and excuses but when you are committed ... you will do whatever it takes."*

This book can provide a big turning point in your

life. Not just by reading it, by applying it's wisdom. So, the first question I have for you is ... *Are you ready?*

When Josh left my home after eight hours of talking, learning, planning and committing to his goals, I had zero doubt that his ability to focus like a laser on exactly what he wanted would result in him becoming the number one franchise in the world in his industry. He was committed to achieving his biggest goals and dreams and so the question now goes to you, the reader:

Are you interested or are you committed to creating the biggest version of your life and achieving all of your life's goals and dreams?

If you are committed, read this book every week and follow what Josh shares. It will transform you and your results.

— JOHN ASSARAF
Chairman & CEO
NeuroGym | MyNeuroGym.com

PREFACE

I HAVE A GREAT FATHER, Peter Liske. Many of you may know him from *Deadliest Catch,* Discovery Channel's most famous series. He was the captain of the fishing vessel *Lady Alaska* in Season One which aired ten episodes in 2005. He is also my hero.

I spent seven summers on the fishing boat with my dad and there was one particular summer when I was about 12 years old that I remember well. I was helping my uncle get the boat ready for the upcoming salmon season; in the winter we would catch crab, anywhere from king crab, to blue crab, to snow crab. We were working with the ropes and I was walking backwards when all of sudden I fell down into the crab pot—the hole where they keep the crab and the salmon, probably about 15–16 feet deep. Luckily I fell onto a ladder and slid all the way down to the bottom so no major injuries. But I can still remember my heart racing so fast I thought it would explode, and it was still pounding as I frantically climbed back up the ladder to the main deck.

My story may be like many of you where you have fallen or been knocked down—maybe it's a business, maybe it's a relationship—but I'm here to encourage you and to let you know that great things await you as you climb back up the ladder. All it takes is one step, *one rung at a time* to ascend your ladder to success.

• • •

It is my hope that each and every one of you can find your correct ladder that can take you far in life as I did. And it is with that heartfelt intent that I want to share seven things—seven steps—that I believe are the secrets, or keys, regarding my ladder of success starting as just a sales person, then moving up into management, leadership, and my own franchise.

—JOSH LISKE

INTRODUCTION

I BELIEVE FIRST AND FOREMOST that my story of success started with me getting into direct selling at the age of eighteen. I had just came back from a summer of fishing with my dad in Alaska. I had worked hard and I think I made about $4,500, which was an incredible amount of money at the time for a summer job.

I had just finished high school and was already thinking about my future. I knew that I wanted to be living on my own instead of living with friends or family and I needed a job. I was used to making good money in Alaska and had grown up with my father making great money so I knew that I didn't want a minimum wage job.

My dad and I always talked about me joining him in the fishing business but now I wasn't so sure. I enjoyed the ocean and I loved Alaska, but I disliked having my father gone anywhere from seven to nine months a year. The money was excellent and we had a great lifestyle but I never really wanted to go into it, never had the passion for it like my dad did.

My father is from the Cleveland, Ohio, area. He played some college football and then went into the military and served in Vietnam. After the war he and my mom Kelli moved to Anacortes, Washington. He was working as a carpenter when I was born and shortly thereafter got into commercial fishing, starting as a cook and a deckhand, then becoming an engineer and a skipper and one of the most successful crab fishermen the Bering Sea has ever seen over the last 30 years.

In 1993, there was a TV series called "Those Who Dare" and it was about the 13 most dangerous jobs in the world that aired on

The Discovery Channel. They wanted to air an episode about the dangers of being on a boat in the Bering Sea in the midst of some of the coldest and stormiest waters on earth and they chose to feature my dad out of all the skippers. And I appeared on that episode as well. My dad would coach half our season in football practice and they had me on that show where we were walking up the football field up with his arm around me.

My folks divorced when I was 13 and it was by far the hardest thing I ever went through as a child. Less than a year later my father married my stepmother, this amazing woman of God and mom who had three children. Not long after that I learned that my dad had fathered another son so I also have a half-brother that is four years older than me. I had kind of heard about him but I didn't want to accept it, that was difficult. So as a young teenager I went from a family of three children and a mom and dad, to a new step-mom and seven children within a 12-month period.

My father and stepmother were very

involved in the church and we moved to Cincinnati, Ohio. My dad still resides there with his wife and they've been married 23 years. At the time they became interested in foster parenting and that's what later led me to be a foster parent. I speak of that later in the book about how we have a vision to build a children's camp in Costa Rica. And since moving to Ohio, my father and stepmother have adopted 9 children so that makes me one of 16 children: eight boys, eight girls and I am the fourth oldest. The most I ever lived with was 11 children at one time.

When I was 16 years old, I wanted to move back to Anacortes and play sports and finish my high school career on a high note. I've always been on good teams and played every sport from bowling and golf, to football, basketball and baseball. We placed first in State in bowling, first in State in soccer, and second in State in basketball. When I returned to Washington I lived with family friends and I was going to be the starting point guard on Anacortes High School basketball team.

But when I was 17, I had to have knee surgery and then another knee surgery—and by the time I was 18 I had three knee surgeries. But it wasn't the surgery that really caused a major challenge and an overwhelming feeling of defeat—it was the State of Washington. When school officials found out that I moved back without my parents, they said I couldn't play sports that year. This absolutely crushed me emotionally and was probably the second-hardest thing I ever went through besides my parents' divorce. I appealed their decision to the highest level the State of Washington has ever allowed and they still said no. So here I was, back in my home town without my parents, still feeling some scars from parents' divorce, I was living with friends, and then I find out that I can't play high school sports! I wasn't sure what my life had in store for me or how to reinvent my plans going forward. *What was I going to do now?*

The day that I got back from Alaska, which was the middle of July 1997, I opened a newspaper and started looking for a job. There was an ad that caught my eye and it said "Shampoo 12 to 15 carpets, make up to $750 a week." I remember thinking: *Okay, shampooing carpets out of the back of the van—I need a job, I can do that!* I interviewed with a gentleman in a restaurant not too far from my house in Anacortes and the next day I went to his office, which was about 20 minutes away the next city over in Mount Vernon, Washington. He showed me the product for about two hours and let me know that I could make it a career and he offered me a job.

The very next day I started with my business in direct selling and based off sales my first week I made $625. My original plan was to work a few months and then start Skagit Valley Community College in Mount Vernon, Washington, which is the town adjacent to Anacortes. I had always dreamed of going to school to learn physical therapy or sports medicine. But when I got to college on that first day I basically walked in the classroom and before the class even started I turned around and walked out.

I realized that I was already starting to excel at my business. It had started out as a summer job but instead of shampooing carpets out of the back of the van I was in direct sales and selling a high-end product that retailed for almost $2,000 US dollars. I found myself making excellent money and saw the opportunity at this business. I even had a week of over $1,000 in seven days worth of work—I found myself making more money than my professors! So I dropped out of school and decided to give my new job a serious try. I knew that it was going to take a lot of hard work and dedication but I had seen other people doing it and if other people could do it—*I could do it!* I would give it a good three months, and if it didn't work out then I'd go back to school the following semester.

My sales leader at the time was driving a nice car, had a beautiful house, had a beautiful wife, and, a beautiful family, and that's the lifestyle I always desired. I figured if I worked hard and, based off the program of this company, I could achieve my goal a lot faster than if I was in school for four years and then another four years or so getting settled into a career. And lo and behold, it only took me 3½ years to become a branch manager, which at that time, we did over $1 million our second year in business. I had to move 80 miles away, another ladder for me to climb, but after roughly nine years I had become the highest level in my company direct selling. I moved two different states away, met my wife and nothing has been the same ever since I met the ladder of my dreams.

• • •

I literally got into my business 18 years ago by accident and here we are today and we've reached the number one spot in the world, the number one franchise in over 55 nations. There are roughly 1,500 offices and last year we were number one. And we just recently won the "Chairman's Cup," which is like winning the Heisman Trophy or MVP in our company. Our products are sold in over 50 nations throughout the world and they take the top six distributors for the contest period and they vote among the peers. There are about 60–64 people that vote, including spouses, from the top offices throughout the world. And they voted us—my wife Gina and I—as the Chairman Cup 2015 winners. This has been a great journey for me and there have been so many blessings and so much I want to share with you that I have learned along the way …

1

BURNING DESIRE

STEP NUMBER ONE on the ladder of success is *burning desire.* My franchise didn't start off as well as others—I only had roughly $8,200, plus I had to move two states away—but I was inspired because I knew in my heart where I was going.

I believe that clarity is one of the keys to a burning desire; when you know what you want and you are crystal clear on the vision of your goals and dreams.

I learned at a young age that our words have power. I remember when I was fifteen I wanted to start varsity basketball, even though I was just a freshman. It was all I could think about. I would wake up 15-20 minutes early and go dribble the basketball one or two miles before school every single day. I lived in Ohio at the time so there was some very cold mornings. This morning ritual really made a difference with my conditioning, and it also increased my skill and helped my performance.

I knew that I wasn't the fastest or the strongest, nor was I the tallest or the most athletic, but one thing I had above all the rest was a **burning desire.** My dad always told me that there's always someone out there working harder than you and I never wanted to be that someone out there that was working harder than me.

I started training with wind sprints to make myself faster and stronger; I had heard that over time it helps build your body's speed, power and endurance. So at a young age I became very focused on my goal and learned all I had to do was to dig deep and I would find that burning desire to make the team and be their number one player. It's the passion and burning desire that lights the flame.

I began proclaiming that I was going to play on the varsity team; I kept saying it over and over and over again. I wasn't being cocky, I wasn't arrogant. I said it with humility and I would say it often, and I said it as if it would happen— that I believed it would happen—and that I would rise to the occasion. And these words of proclamation helped me reach my goal of making the varsity team my freshman year.

There are many different stories of burning desire throughout my life when things weren't going so well and I wanted to succeed so badly. I would keep doing and keep going; I would push and I wouldn't give up and I became the only a freshman on the varsity team. When others would fall off the bandwagon, I would continue to show up. I do believe that eighty percent of success is *just showing up.* It's amazing what you can learn when you continue to show up but it's even more incredible what you can accomplish when you're hit with a burning desire.

YOU MUST SEE IT TO BELIEVE IT

A few things that have really helped in our business is a thing called "vision boards." Not long ago we were on the verge of becoming "Golden Circle," the highest level of achievement in our company and we wanted it. We only had 15 days left to reach this milestone and still needed about $80,000. On top of that the weather was difficult and there were so many obstacles ahead of us. So I brought in a friend, a leader and a mentor that taught us a strategy of the Navy Seals where you visualize for long periods at a time.

That's when the idea of vision boards hit me and I decided we should try them on a corporate basis. I used a large 4x6-foot whiteboard in my sales meeting. There were roughly 80 people in there and as I spoke I wrote what we needed in the center of the vision board. I didn't write down the $80,000 dollar amount—I wrote down the number of sales which would get us to the $80,000 mark. That amount was a very large number and quite a stretch for us at the time.

I went around the room and I started asking people, *"How can we get there, working backwards? To reach this number, what do we need to do? How many hours do we need to put in? How many prospects do we need to see?"* And by the time the board was done we had about 50 to 60 ideas of how to reach that goal.

We also decided to make smaller vision boards for each department in the company. We would look at those vision boards every night and throughout the day; they were on the walls and various places in the office, and at home on the refrigerator door, the bathroom mirror—anywhere we could look in order to motivate us and increase our burning desire. Every minute of every day, it was exhausting and I can't tell you how many times I wanted to give up. But we reached our goal and we each walked away with an extreme sense of accomplishment and pride.

Part of burning desire is taking a risk, or perhaps I should say calculated risk versus just a risk; they have to be orchestrated, they have to be on purpose, and they have to be intentional.

CLARITY IN OBJECTIVE

I believe that clarity is one of the keys to a burning desire; where you know what you want (some people say *"laser focused"*) and you are crystal clear on the vision of your goals. You have a dream and it is without a shadow of a doubt that you have the laser-beam focus you will need to penetrate your goal. No matter what the obstacle is, what the weather is or whatever storm you may be going through—at the end of the day when you are laser focused and possess a burning desire that you can find the strength to meet any challenge.

TIME FOR A RESET

I believe that climbing the ladder once you have clarity will bring simplicity. And you can help facilitate that by writing down what you want, what your goals are; it can be on a company vision board or on a simple notepad with your wife and children.

One thing we do every single month in the company is called "a month at a glance." This gives us a 30-day snapshot of upcoming goals and events. In addition to that, we have a six-month snap, a twelve-month snap and a five-year snap. Now, we don't do this once in a while; *we do this every month at the beginning of the month!* This allows us to reset our goals, reset our desire, and get a clear understanding where we're going.

What is the desire that you want? *What ladder are you climbing?*

Many of the greatest lessons I've learned about burning desire actually come after the miracle; once you accomplish your goal, *what do you do next?* One of the keys to having a burning desire and reaching the top of your ladder is that you have to be *a person of reset.* What I mean by that is, once or even before you reset your goal you have to immediately be thinking about your next goal. Many times I've seen people work hard and hit their goal and then the next month they have a much worse month.

So the key is to reset your goals, to reset your desire; to have the clarity of where you're going not only this month but next month and each month after that. This is why it's so very important to have clarity, it's one of the keys to cultivating burning desire.

I know a little about risk and this is one of my favorite stories. At the age of 22, I was a very young man and had the opportunity to move up the ladder, I had a desire to move up. But the territory I was in was already covered so I would have to move. Well, I'm from the small town, an island, and I could not envision myself as a city boy. But, when opportunity arose I jumped on it, once again because of my burning desire. My company and I relocated and moved 80 miles away; me—*and this is no joke*—and the worst salesman in our entire organization.

I decided to teach this young man some of the business principles I had learned and I gave him a month-at-a-glance calendar. He mentioned he wanted a new car so I asked him, "What would you need to do to reach that goal?" We wrote a plan for the car he wanted and then sat down to figure out how many presentations he would need to do; how many sales he needs to get; and how much profit he wanted to make. And guess what? *He went from being our worst salesman and within the very next month he became our best salesman.* Just like that!

I think a lot of people have potential in them, but a good leader will find greatness in their people. I knew this young man had potential but I would need to help pull it out of him and help with his sense of direction. Everything rises and falls on leadership.

DEFINING YOUR GOAL

Goals are important. In goal setting you have daily goals and you can have hourly goals and minute goals. But in our business, we break it down into a couple different categories: *Daily goals* which give you a 12-hour window; then *sprint goals* which would be a three-day goal. Oftentimes our workweek is six days so we would need to do two sprints a week. And we would also need to do *weekly goals, monthly goals, three-month goals, six-month goals,* and then a *five-year plan of action and goals.*

I often suggest you start with small goals. A bunch of small goals add up to a big goal, or a big win. A lot of victories equal an over-all victory. So it will actually help you to have a lot of small wins in the beginning. It's like in boxing, you have the heavy-weight boxer, all the way down to junior boxing; a heavy-weight boxer can sustain a lot more, they can endure a lot more. Often in business as you look forward, you've got to forecast— or in a marriage you have to forecast. It's about being passionate, forecasting, and visualizing; those are three of the keys that helped propel my burning desire.

Another key to reaching a burning desire is *working backwards* so I often suggest breaking it down into manageable pieces to help it become easier. For example, one of our top sales reps for the entire quarter (he was number one in nine different states) said, "Josh, here's what I want to do. Here's what I want to accomplish." We sat down and created a 90-day time-frame and then worked backwards. "How many presentations, how many prospects will you need to see?" I asked. It was quite interesting at the end of the 90 days. Yes, he was already a top salesman, but the underlying principle was that he wanted to be Number One, he desired to be in first place—and he succeeded.

• • •

There is something valuable in taking risk. There's something valuable in having clarity and there's something valuable in knowing exactly what you want. So, no matter what ladder you're climbing I encourage you—once you have clarity—to work backwards. Write your goals down and know exactly how you're going to get there.

One of the biggest keys to success is burning desire, and to share one of the greatest quotes I have used throughout my entire career:

"When the desire parallels the goal, anything is possible."

2

KNOWLEDGE

S TEP NUMBER TWO on the ladder of success is
knowledge. People often say knowledge is powerful. But one thing I've learned over the years is
that "applied knowledge" is even more powerful.

For example, a good friend of mine got a degree
in Criminal Justice. He is very successful but he's not
practicing law, he's not even in law enforcement. You
can have any diploma or any degree but if you don't

have massive application then the knowledge will be irrelevant. I never went to college. I didn't go to school to learn about business, I was self-taught, a real hands-on learner. I was in the trenches there learning every single day what to say, when to say it, how to say it. So once again, it's applied knowledge that is so powerful.

It's also very important to have "product knowledge." In my career I've sat in a sales meeting six days a week now for eighteen years; I'm talking hundreds of hours of sales meeting. Sometimes I lead the meeting and other times we have sales trainers come in. And over the years I've found it's the hands-on participation that's a very relevant key to product knowledge.

EXPANDING YOUR PRODUCT KNOWLEDGE

One of the more significant aspects to learning product knowledge is really very simple: bring a notebook and a pen! I've seen so many people attend a seminar or a rally and they don't take notes. It's really imperative that we take notes so we can help retain the information, and then also review the notes within 72 hours; either by re-reading them, or writing them out again. So often your notes can cover a 45-minute session of education time, and then when you go back and you take out 3, 5 or 10 suggestions, hone them down to what you think is the most important and re-write your notes, you have a powerful source and reference of increasing knowledge.

A simple formula that applies here and can help with your success as well—*listen, believe, and follow.* You need to listen to the instructor, you need to believe what he is saying, and then the most difficult part—and I think the important part—is you have to follow through with what they're saying. For example they might be talking about voice inflection with the customer, so if you can repeat word-for-word, but also voice-inflection-for-voice-inflection that will tremendously help your knowledge.

I also believe that you need "people knowledge," or people skills. What we read, what we listen to, even who we hang out with—those are the big three I call, "Own Your Improvement of Product Knowledge."

GROWING YOUR PERSONAL DEVELOPMENT

While product knowledge is certainly important, what is even more important is *personal development;* they go hand in hand. As I learn the product, I get better at what I do. If you know the product very well but you're not growing there's no way that you're going to improve your skills or improve your income. However, on the flip side as you learn your product and increase your mindset you'll begin thinking like a champion and you'll want to hang around champions.

You've probably heard the old saying that "communication is everything." Well, did you know that 55 percent of communication is actually body language and 38 percent is voice inflection? That leaves 7 percent—the words that we use are only 7 percent! That means that the most important aspect of your communication is your body language. So I had to learn how to be animated and how to communicate and deal with customers.

We have two products in my industry: one is our product and the other product is the *people*. So I learned that when I got good with the people, my sales went up. I encourage you today that no matter what ladder you're on as you get better relationships, they'll become stronger. As you become more powerful in whatever industry that you're in, you will see it grow.

Just as the product knowledge grows, also the knowledge of you growing will make a big difference.

Three different times throughout my career I have put myself on a permanent program of self-improvement, three different times that I can recall as very defining moments. Such as my iPod phase where I played self-improvement audiobooks all night long for a 90-day period. I would fall asleep and then wake up each morning listening to them.

What this did for me consciously, but most importantly subconsciously, was a great time of growth and prosperity. I saw my income growing and my product knowledge growing. I would listen to various CDs on growth, attitude development and goal setting. This was a very important time of acquiring the knowledge I would need to prosper. And it was the subconscious part of the learning that wound up helping me consciously over the next few days and weeks because I would be spitting things out I didn't even know that I had inside me from this permanent program of self-improvement.

I began to see immediate results from these programs of intensity that helped me to reach for the next level. I remember when I was just starting my franchise in California and how much I wanted to improve quickly. I was making the shift from an employee to an employer and within a matter of short 12 months I was able to get promoted to the highest level in my company. Without the intensity of this self-improvement program there's no way that I could have been able to get promoted that quickly.

KNOW YOUR STRENGTHS — IMPROVE YOUR WEAKNESSES

If you want to become an expert, you have to know your strengths. People often say, "Focus on your weaknesses," but what I found is that it is better to *focus on your strengths while improving your weaknesses.*

In general, people don't care how much you know until they know how much you care. So part of your success will come from just caring about people, and then knowing that people really do like to be led. It's imperative that you first ascertain and acknowledge your strengths. Then once you pinpoint the strengths you need to keep adding to that, kind of like adding kindling or firewood to the fire to keep it burning. Then slowly you can start to focus on your weaknesses and there's a lot that can come from this approach. I call it "positive praise" where we praise people, encourage them, give them a smile and a high-five. That can go a long way when you're encouraging a potential recruit or someone that's new in your company and you want to help bring out their personal best.

When you're consistently praising one of your people, then it's not as painful when you talk to them about some areas that might need improvement. I call it the "sandwich effect"—you praise someone and then offer constructive criticism, and then you praise them again. So you might mention something they did well and then say, "Hey, by the way, I think we can correct this one thing here," and then close with "Let's go get 'em, tiger!"

No matter what you're going through, I encourage you to get a book, listen to a CD, go to a seminar. Almost every major decision I made in my life was at a rally or a seminar where people of great multitude were there—being around a room full of *leaders and achievers* can be very motivating! So, I encourage you to find a CD, a tape or a book; attend seminars and workshops—listen and learn, and broaden your tent post, your tent pegs.

I also place a high value on good mentorship, both as a student and a steward. When I first moved back to Seattle as a brand new distributor, which was the highest level, I knew first-hand the power and the value of mentorship. I've always had a mentor who was my direct distributor. And then when I became a distributor I realized its kind of lonely at the top. I found myself in church several times a week and learned the church that I attended had a great business mindset. They even had a marketplace ministry, so I often found myself in their meetings. I was attracted to the qualities of one particular leader and sought him out for questions and answers. Now that I had achieved a certain level of success I found myself completely on my own and knew I needed to connect with someone to help guide me.

I wasn't looking to him for his business experience because he was never in my business, but he mentored me spiritually, physically, and emotionally. And then shortly later I met my wife, and I would seek counsel with him because he had a successful marriage, a successful business, and was a successful leader.

Actually, I feel it's important to have a good mentor both in the business world and also in your personal world. Every leader also needs a good doctor, a good pastor, a good CPA, a good business mentor, a good personal mentor, and a good attorney. So I think, if you have those six you are going to have a successful life.

It helps to have a wide range of people that you can pull from for specific situations. What makes a good coach is not necessarily their ability, of course that's important, but its often who they surround themselves with. So I think that the people I've surrounded myself with have made a huge impact. They say the six closest people to you will determine your income and your outcome; pretty much everything you know about somebody is to look at their five closest friends!

The mind is a very powerful thing so as we increase our thinking, and as we increase our way of doing things, we increase our knowledge of the product. Climbing your ladder becomes simpler when you understand these principles. And these principles of knowledge also go hand-in-hand with the principle of *growing yourself on purpose.*

When you're green, you're growing.
When you're ripe, you're rotten.

• • •

I can recall early in my career when I was turning 19. It was my birthday weekend and I had made plans with all my friends to attend a Dave Matthews concert, which was roughly a three-hour drive away.

It was a Friday afternoon and I was driving with a guy that I was leading. The majority of my friends and colleagues were already heading for the concert. While most of my friends were in college and now enjoying a long summer break, I had already been hard at work in the business world for about 15 months. I had made it to team leader and was in charge of one to two other guys and now had some responsibility in the office. In our business, we work when people are home, so we capitalize on Saturday and Sunday and, of course, evenings.

I called my business leader, who was also my mentor, to let him know that I was about halfway into my trip and I recall him saying, "I think you should turn around." *Not* something I wanted to do—*not* how I wanted to celebrate my birthday! But one thing I had learned is that you don't want to miss a Saturday, that's the money day; the most important day to be at the office.

Something inside of me knew I had to turn around. I knew instinctively that one of the keys to growing yourself is to *listen, believe, and follow.* Many times people listen, many times people believe. But the "key" here is *you have to have to follow through.*

I realized I had made a bad business decision to take off and attend the concert, I had made a mistake. So I had to apologize to the guy I was leading because he wanted to go there as well. We had convinced ourselves that it would be okay because we'd work a little along the way, which would have been a disaster. But something inside me, a gut feeling really, knew the right thing to do would be to turn around so we could be in the office early Saturday morning. I remember at the time a lot of my friends made fun of me and were thinking, "You're working too much, why can't you skip a weekend?"

One thing I know that my father always taught me is that you have to sacrifice, and so I definitely sacrificed by missing the concert. But I made the right decision and I went back to the office and had a great weekend.

I think being successful is a process. Since my boss had risen to the top level in our industry, he knew what it would take to get there so he absolutely was leading me and guiding me when he encouraged me to return. But, then again, I also had to be coachable; throughout my career I've always been very coachable.

Sometimes you have to be under authority before you can have authority.

• • •

My Dave Matthews weekend became a pivotal moment where I climbed to a higher level of commitment in my professional career. Looking back, it was absolutely a lesson moment and I have learned over the years that you need to pick and choose your battles as you climb your ladder of success. I encourage you to separate yourself from the pack, learn who you are as a person and what you want. Many times in my life I have had to make sacrifices as far as the product knowledge goes, same with the personal development. I learned product knowledge, I made difficult choices, I worked on my personal development. And if you do the same thing, anything is possible.

3

INTENSITY

S TEP NUMBER THREE on the ladder of success
is *intensity.* I believe every ladder of success re-
quires a season of intensity—you'll find that you
can climb whatever ladder, whatever challenge, whatever mountain you're facing.

There was a period of time early in my career, I had
been working in my business for about two years, when
I was at a crossroads and I really needed to make a

decision about my future. As I contemplated my choices I realized that I had never fully invested myself nor really given my current industry everything I had. So, I decided to do a *push month,* an entire month of extreme dedication where I would push myself—I mean really push myself—every day for 31 straight days.

Remember, this is step is about "intensity" and as the term implies, I decided to eliminate all excuses and put myself on a permanent program of self-improvement. I told my friends. I told my girlfriend. I even told my goldfish. I announced to everyone that I was absolutely 100% committed. You're wondering what was I committed to? ***I was committed to my commitment.***

People often say I am committed in my work but I believe you have to go one step further and commit to your commitment. So, I made a commitment to work 31 days in a row, full-out with everything I had within me. From bell to bell—from morning, noon and night. The result? *It transformed me, it gave me new self-image. And it gave me a new vision, a new perspective and a new sense of purpose.*

After 31 days I was completely changed. They say it takes 21 days to form a new habit. So around day number 21, maybe day number 22, it actually got to be fun because by then it became a habit. I don't believe you ever acquire a new habit; I think you replace habits. So what I did was replace some of these bad habits with new habits—new habits that gave me confidence, that gave me fortitude. These new habits offered many things that I didn't have before.

I learned more about myself in that 31-day intensity push than I had learned in all the previous 24 months. A lot of things came out of me, a lot of qualities and abilities that I didn't know I had. *What a nice surprise!* I encourage you to challenge yourself to a 7-day, 14-day or 31-day intensity push. There are so many rewards awaiting you.

MOTIVATION

A wish or desire is something you talk about, and a goal is something that is written down and defined, a specific goal. But I believe a visual is just as important as writing it down and would often pin my goals on the bathroom mirror and the dashboard to the company work vehicles.

One thing I love about the world of sales is that every day is a new day. Even though you might have had a bad day yesterday, it doesn't mean you have to have a bad day today. I love every Monday because it is a new week, and I love the first of every month because it is a new month. The nice thing is you can reset yourself, and I think its very important that you know where you are going, just like a ship on a rudder—you can take the best navy ship or the best fishing vessel or the fastest ski boat but if you take out the rudder then its no longer effective, and I believe that's the same thing with humanity. It can have the most potential, the most talent, but if you don't have a specific direction or a goal then it can become a wasted talent.

I'm often asked how you can motivate others to commit to a period of intensity. I believe *leaders lead from the front, and bosses tell you what to do.* I've always been an action leader so I always lead from the front.

I have learned there are three types of motivation:

1. *Carrot stick,* which is the least important form of motivation. It entails an incentive such as a new car or a bonus check or a promotion.

2. *Fear,* which is the worst form of motivation. Some coaches scream and some coaches motivate, there are different styles of coaching. For me, fear motivation translates to "I need to

pay my rent and haven't met my income quota," or "I don't want to lose the respect of my peers" and that will help drive my performance.

3. **Internal motivation,** which is the best form of motivation. It brings with it a couple of things, but number one is personal development. Also key is self-image, so if an individual or a team can improve their self-imagine then you're going to find a lot of times they can be more internally motivated. *When you can find it from within, anything is possible.*

It's also important to surround yourself with people that help your vision. For example, my wife has been a great cheerleader, there's only one time in our entire marriage that she complained regarding my long hours working. The opposite of a cheerleader would be a "monkey on the back," I've seen so many good people lose a dream or be knocked down because of the monkey-on-the-back, and I call them dream-stealers. Its often the loved ones, its often the people closest to us, they become dream-stealers. When you talk about winning that incentive trip, or getting another promotion, you need to be aware of the monkey-on-the-back. You are trying to make something of yourself and if someone close to you is finding fault or holding you back, that's not going to help. *Either you are wind in my sail, or an anchor in my tail.*

Another thing that has really helped me, uplift and transfer me, is what we call "international sellathon." We have it four times a year and in the early stages of my career I found myself mesmerized by the results where we would often have double or triple or even quadruple our best day. We would wake up early and we would start earlier and we'd work later. But it is not just about working an extra two hours or three hours each day. We added massive intensity for the entire company with over 55 nations going for one push where we'd have prizes up front for the guys to earn that day. This is one way to help you with your intensity workouts, your intensity growth, and this is a great example of carrot motivation.

A SEASON OF INTENSITY

As you continue to go from favor to favor or from prosperity to prosperity, whatever you may be looking at, I encourage you that at these windows of opportunity it's very important to pick and choose your battles. There's a time to rest and there's a time to push. When you are a go-getter, when you're career minded and you're really looking for that ladder of success, you'll find the ladder.

There are different levels of rock climbing. For example, you could do just regular mountain hiking; you could do rock climbing or you can do intense rock climbing. Not everyone is interested in doing this because you need a different type of shoe and a different type of harness. It will separate you from being a star, to a superstar. When you can find those windows of opportunities, moments where you understand that the ladder needs to be more inclined, there's going to be a different issue, a different season.

As you make the sacrifice, one of the keys to success is to get great people behind you to encourage and motivate you. You might even be pushing yourself—it is a steep ladder—but when you've got someone down there cheering you on, pushing you upwards during your time of intensity, truly the sky's the limit! It's certainly been a big key to my success that I've had through my wife and other mentors. As they encourage you to climb your ladder *anything* is possible.

If you can focus for 7 days, 14 days, or like in my case 31 days, it will transform your life. Once again, I believe the season of intensity is ladder-step number three.

> Football practice, I can still remember those "two-a-days"—and in our school we even had "three-a-days." These practices are officially called "training camp," but many refer to it as *hell week*, a few hellish weeks of twice-daily workouts at the hottest time of the year designed to get players in shape for the upcoming season.
>
> Believe it or not, I used to actually like the two- and three-a-days because I understood the concept: "If we push hard now, it's going to be easier later." I really don't want to use the term *easy* here because there is certainly nothing easy about hell week. What I understood was that the coaches were just trying to condition us because if we practice intensively now, it will be more *simple* once we're on the playing field.

Training camp is a time where you need to lay it all out in the field. Some say that *you play like you practice.*

And one thing I learned at an early age is that intensity is really burning desire, and if you have that burning desire it really shows in practice. Whether you're in the game or out of the game—you need to treat everything like you're in the game.

Maybe at the office, you're the first one there in the morning and last one to leave at night. Just because you're scheduled to work eight hours, why not work nine hours? Why not be truly productive? Why not be a half hour early, and a half hour late? Once again, we're talking about climbing up the ladder of success and there is a season for *intensity.*

It's not about the miles ... it's not about the yards. Winning is often about the *inches.*

• • •

There are many horse races that are won by the nose of a horse. Or like in golf, you might win by one stroke. You become 10× or 3× the earner because you're just a little bit better. I believe it's these moments of intensity that are going to help you be just a bit better. We're not talking about a lot better here—we're talking about being

59

a little better here and a little bit better there, and at the end of the day that will be a key factor in helping you climb your ladder of success.

4

ATTITUDE

S TEP NUMBER FOUR on climbing your ladder of success is *attitude.* This is probably my favorite of the steps. I learned at a young age from my father that having a positive attitude will take you far in life. We always say in our business, *"We'll take someone with a good attitude over someone that's talented."*

Attitude is something you develop. I have a beautiful wife and three beautiful children and one thing we teach in our household is attitude. One thing we say about attitude is: _Attitude Triumphantly Takes Individuals Through Unbelievable Difficulties Every Day._ No matter what you're faced with, we can all choose to have a good attitude or a bad attitude.

It's not what happens to us,
it's how we handle what happens to us
that's important.

POSITIVE MENTAL ATTITUDE

Another thing our business is built on—that I built my franchise on—is "PMA," which stands for "Positive Mental Attitude." **_Positive people get positive results._** We can choose to smile or we can choose to frown. Part of just being happy and being positive is our body language, just a simple smile can do the trick. This is a key, a trait, that you have to learn how to do. No matter what the setbacks are, you can smile. You can make that part of your attitude arsenal.

For example, one of the presidents at our bank says, "Josh, you always have a good attitude, no matter what you're going through. That's what I love about you." I think that's something that I trained in myself, something I developed along the way because the first 11 months of my business were not easy. I was young and eager—*and it was difficult*—but once I learned how to control my attitude, I then had control of my destiny. An analogy would be like "water on a ducks back." I didn't let the customer effect me any longer, I didn't let my girlfriend effect me, a situation, a cancellation, a problem deal, or a setback. Once I learned and understood the psychology behind that and learned how to control it, I found myself quite a bit more successful.

Learning how to overcome rejections or setbacks comes from maturing in personal growth, personal development. I've learned many things over the years by studying the psychology of behavior, the psychology of attitude and the psychology of goal-setting. I'm not saying I've never been thrown off the horse, but its pretty much consistent no matter what happens to me at this point, that my attitude is pretty solid and not easily effected.

As you're climbing your ladder, learn how to control the attitude. Learn what to say, learn what not to say. Not only is what we say important, but also what we hear and what we receive. It's important how we think and it's also important how we receive things.

Several things have helped me over the years and one of them is "attitude stickers." You can put an attitude banner in your office or you can write an attitude on your mirror. These are subconscious things that can help you and there are many different things you can do reinforce positive attitude. But how do we *train* or *control* our attitude? By the books we read, by the tapes we listen to, and by the people you associate with. Some people have "stinking thinking" so it's important to pay attention to the friends we choose, the people we associate with. I choose to hang around people that are positive. I choose to hang around people that are optimistic.

So many times in my career I have had to make a sacrifice. One of my dearest stories is about my father, my biggest hero. He has been my hero my whole life but for about four years we did not speak. It wasn't that my father wasn't positive because he's a very positive man and that's something I learned from him, but he became kind of negative about my career, about where I was going. Now, of course, he's so proud of me and he's so happy for what I've done and accomplished. But even though he was my father, my hero, there was period of time that I had to separate myself from him because I had to *learn how to control my attitude.*

I also had to learn how to *protect* my attitude. See, that's important—you have to guard your mind, you have to guard your thoughts. It's one thing to be positive when things are good, when good things are happening. *But what happens when things aren't so good?* I often refer to it as the difference between a *professional* and *amateur.* An amateur is positive and has a good attitude when things are going good—a professional is positive no matter the circumstances or the setbacks. This is one of the keys that I've learned in how to control my attitude.

Another thing about attitude, and just the way of thinking and how this whole thing happens. Your true friends will stay true friends forever and ever. As I just mentioned, there was a long time where not only did I not speak to my father, but to many of my high school friends. I grew up in a small community and we were all close; we played sports together, we grew up together. But, I was on my journey and when I was climbing my ladder of success, many of us didn't talk for a time—for months, for years. But my true friends, they came to my wedding. My true friends, I went to their wedding. When things are very important, life events that are important, your friends will be there.

THE FIVE "P's"

Another way to control your attitude is not only by learning through tapes, books and CDs but through self-meditation. Many times one of the keys is to just quiet yourself down, to get a plan. You'll often hear that a businessman or businesswoman knows how their next month will go based off their plan. This correlates to the infamous Five P's: _Proper Planning Prevents Poor Performance._ If you can learn how to have good performance, this will help your attitude. If you can learn how to be an achiever, this will give you a good attitude. I believe that making the right decisions is one of the secrets to having a good attitude.

When you do what you're _supposed_ to do—not what you _want_ to do—you feel good about yourself. You can keep your chest high, you can walk with confidence, you walk with integrity. So, I encourage you as you're going forward, hang round the right people and focus on things that make you money. Focus on things that winners do because *quitters never win, and winners never quit.*

Learning to have a good attitude is imperative but it's the "not giving up" that is by far one of the biggest keys to success. How do you not give up you ask? You stay focused on your goal, you stay *laser beam focused.* When you know that, it's easy to have a good attitude. When you know where you're going, it's easy to have a good attitude.

Here's a little analogy that might help: My father's a commercial fisherman in Alaska. He has a beautiful boat. I've been on it many times, but I can assure you if you take away the ruder of that boat, that boat is no longer efficient, that boat no longer has direction.

A positive attitude is like a rudder on the boat. It'll give you direction. It will give you clarity. It will give you vision, and it can take you anywhere.

The words we use are so powerful. The words we speak are so powerful. Many of my successes, whether it's my freshman year on the basketball team, or rising to the top of my company, I would speak with a good attitude. I would declare with a good attitude. This gave me confidence; this gave me insight: *When the attitude is right, it makes the perseverance easy.*

Attitude and perseverance—they go hand in hand. When it's challenging, it's not challenging to me. When it's challenging to the other person, it's easier to me. Everything is in comparison. Many times I've had trainees in my business that came in and they left saying, "This is too difficult or this is hard." But one thing I've always told myself is, "It's not as hard as this person doing this, or this person doing that."

Another thing about attitude that will help you is learning to be a "steady-eddy," they're the ones that stay the course, the ones that have a consistent attitude throughout the whole week, the whole day, the whole month, the whole year.

My father has one of the most dangerous jobs in the world, he works in the Bering Sea with the ice and the weather. Because he had a good attitude, he loves it. It became easy for him. For him it is not difficult. On your ladder of success there might be many people who say this is difficult, but when you're focused, have the right attitude and stay the course, this concept will make it more simple. It will help you find a place in victory as you're moving forward with a positive attitude.

I think the structure of your thoughts plays a big impact on your attitude, that is why it's important to put the right thoughts in—including what you see, what you hear, what you listen to.

> Your thoughts go to your words and
> your words go to your actions,
> your actions go to your habits and
> your habits go to your character, and then
> your character equals your destiny.

• • •

Attitude—it can sink you or help raise you to the top. I encourage you to get the right books; get the right tapes and get the right CDs; go to the right seminars. The mental conditioning through this will allow you to control your attitude, to hang around positive people. As you grow you'll learn it's all about the "Law of Attraction." You're going to find people that are positive, you're going to find people that think like you, and these will be the people that you associate with. They often say, "You can know someone's income bracket by the five closest people in their life." Which five people do you hang out with? Do you need to make a sacrifice? Do you need to make a change?

—✧—

AUTHOR'S NOTE

The sequence of the steps for each chapter is an important part in writing this book. The first four steps we just covered all center around human elements or things that are *intrinsic* to the person or the business man: *Burning Desire, Knowledge, Intensity* and also your *Attitude*. As we climb higher up the ladder, we uncover the secrets of the last three steps of success are a little bit different in that they revolve around *extrinsic factors: The Power of Duplication, Purpose,* and *The Power of God and Prayer.*

I gave considerable thought to the placement of "Purpose" in Chapter Six. To some, the topic of a higher purpose in one's life might seem like a topic of discussion that should go at the end of a book. However, in the context of this book, I wanted to emphasize the importance of purpose and how it can actually become a fuel for what you're doing while you're in the process of reaching what you consider your end game or your goal.

When you have a desire to do well in business, a lot of that desire is driven by making a profit, providing for your family, building something you can pass on to your children, and so on. Those are all what I would call *internal or intrinsic values,* but when purpose comes to light we find ourselves leaving the internal and going to the *external or an extrinsic purpose* of something that's happening outside of the person. Now it's beginning to involve other people. And we're not just talking about the individual businessperson, but how he takes those steps and incorporates them into his every day life and moves through the power of duplication outside of himself into the realm of purpose.

• • •

5

DUPLICATION

S TEP NUMBER FIVE on the ladder of success is
the power of duplication. I love this subject because if it wasn't for the power of duplication,
there's no way that I could have risen my ladder of success. The power of duplication is the key to growing
and expanding your business beyond yourself.

When I first came in my business I had the opportunity to shadow someone and I was able to listen,

watch and see first-hand what the process was about. Once again, you have to *be under authority before you have the authority.* Yes, I've risen up the ladder and I've gained authority but for a long season there, I was under authority. So, the power of duplication is understanding that you've got to be *under* authority, before you ever *get* authority.

BUILDING WIDE

I remember in the beginning of my career in direct sales, I would shadow one of the top sales person in the organization; I would shadow for months and months. We would go out, just he and I, and I would watch him, then he would watch me—for months and months.

This was a great season for me to learn some of that product knowledge I was speaking about earlier. It was also a season of learning to be submissive to the teaching—that you're here to learn, you're here to grow, and you're here to get better. And what I found out that is so cool here is that the key of duplication, once I had learned it and once I owned the information, is that I can teach it. They say that some people are here to teach. Well, I believe there's also another concept: *some people are here to teach how to teach.*

Part of mentorship is understanding, and it goes back to clarity, knowing what you want and then you've got to find a mentor that's willing to mentor you. It's a two-way street though so you, as the mentee, need to be ready to receive.

> The teacher appears when
> the student is ready.

No matter what industry you are in or whether you're a professional athlete or you own a business, it starts with looking and recognizing what you want. When I first moved back to Seattle, I met a couple that had something I wanted; they had a successful business, a successful marriage, they were successful parents—any they became a mentor to me. I believe that is really a direct proportion of *the law of attraction,* which we could touch on probably anywhere in this book because that's a huge aspect of climbing the ladder.

When I became a team leader I oversaw three to four people. Then, I became a branch manager where I would oversee 15–20 people. Now in my current position, I oversee entire departments and serve on a boards of directors. Because of the power of duplication, I can also delegate. I believe that delegating responsibility is one of the keys to *growing wide.*

Yes, I think it's important to be a good salesperson. Yes it's important to be individually good. But I found way more success building wide versus building upward or building downward. Let me give an example here: I could sell X amount of my product, or I could get X amount done. But when you can put together a team—whether it's two people, four people, 20 people, 100 people or over 10,000 people—this is the *power of duplication.*

POWER OF DUPLICATION

Duplication and delegating responsibility can often be a challenge in the beginning because it can be tempting to think, *"This would be faster if I just do it myself. Let me just do it."* But if instead you are willing to say, *"I am going to train this person, I'm going to delegate this area of responsibility and I'm willing to the time to train him rather than do it myself"*—that's the definition of a true leader. Because once you've started down that process of duplication, it becomes a multiplier in your business. You're multiplying your time, which in turn means you're multiplying your revenue and you're multiplying really how high up that ladder that you can climb.

A great example of duplication—and one of my favorites—is about that young gentleman I mentioned in Step One who enrolled in one my courses on direct sales. He was seventeen at the time and had a good attitude. He also had some of the attributes of success, but he had never sold before. He listened and learned and his first few months in sales were okay.

I decided to move him in to the Appointment Center as a canvasser, or in this case a personal assistant. I got him a haircut and I bought him a few nice outfits and on his very first day, he had a prominent level of achievement. The timing was perfect because not only did he get promoted, his self image changed as well.

To the customer he appeared like he was on a higher level, more professional—which is one of the reasons why it's so important to dress for success. His new suit actually changed how he saw himself and his self image. He saw himself on a higher level and so he performed on a higher level and within a couple of years, he was grown-up, had money saved, and on the path of success. He became a branch manager—at the age of 19!—and a few years later he achieved the same position I'm in now. Because of the opportunity and what followed, not only is he good—he's almost equally as good.

Because of the power of duplication, he keeps it simple (we call it the kiss formula for "Keep It Simple Salesperson"). And when asked about his success all he says is, "I just do it like Josh does." *That's the power of duplication.* Of course, at the time I moved him to the Appointment Center I had no idea of his full potential but I quickly learned he was one of those people that wanted more out of life than just to be average. And it really all boils down to just going back to burning desire.

We all know that the basic principle behind duplication is "one plus one equals two." But in this case, the promotion plus a new wardrobe or a different haircut, it is really like "one plus one equals eight, nine, or ten." Currently our office is ranked number one in the world. On last week's report—and here's the best news—this young gentleman, who is now only 23 years old, *is ranked number ten in the world!* So not only are we having success, people around us are having success. It's no good if you're climbing a ladder and you're there alone, all by yourself. I believe the sky's the limit, but I also believe that on top of the ladder there is room for more than just one. That's the beautiful thing about duplication—and if you don't care who gets the credit, we'd all do a lot better.

A VILLAGE

Henry Ford once said, *"Take my factory, take my buildings, but don't take my people."* I believe in building people and the power of duplication—it may be the most powerful step upon the seven steps of building your success because if it's just me, I'm not that good, but "if it's *us,* we're great."

We've all heard the last part of enthusiasm is I-A-S-M or "I Am Sold Myself." When you're sold on building a company, when you're sold on building a team, when you're sold on not only getting the credit, but getting a team effort or championship won, everyone is affected. It's the power of duplication that I believe is one of the keys to success. It's simple really because if it's just me, I can only do so much but *"team together, everyone achieves more."*

Before I got into commercial fishing, I was probably 15, 16 years old and I did construction. If it's just me building a wall, that's not very productive. If you get 2, 3, 4 guys working together the house can go up rather quickly. I believe building a team is like building a house. When the team works in unity—when the team works in one accord, when we're all in one spirit—anything is possible. I can't take any of the credit single-handedly; I've got to give credit to my people, my team members. And that will be easy when you build a team and surround yourself with people better than you in each department.

Remember where I mentioned in Chapter 2 that you need to focus on your strengths and not your weaknesses? I may be the master at one thing but just because I'm strong on one thing, I may not be strong in another. For example, I have a great accountant, a great bookkeeper and a great recruiter. I oversee all these departments but it's important to follow your strengths, to know what you're good at and what you're not so good at, and to surround yourself with people that are experts in their area of expertise. That's part of the key to success and part of the power of duplication.

We all know of the great company Microsoft. I guarantee you that Bill Gates didn't do everything that was necessary to grow that great business. But he's a great visionary and he's a great overseer. So I think as a leader, as you're climbing the steps of your ladder to success, you definitely need to *delegate responsibility.* Delegating responsibility is the power of duplication, and vice versa—duplication comes from delegation. As you delegate people and different departments, you will see them grow.

> People don't care how much you know until they know how much you care.

Another key to duplication is listening—it's very important that we listen to people. It's important that we hear them out, and as we listen to them they are going to tell us how to solve their problems. If we listen to them we can walk with them through their problems. Just as that young kid that came to me when he was seventeen. It wasn't a perfect journey, but it's been a fun journey. It's been a great journey, and he's been able to duplicate the model that we have created and put in place for others. As he's been able to duplicate the international sellathon that we have done—and as he's been able to duplicate in every department that we've done—it is all based off listening, believing and following.

Once again it's the "LBF" formula that I've talked about: "Listen, Believe and Follow." Often people listen, very few believe, and even fewer follow through. *Follow through is a key to duplication.* So, whether you're on the side of delegation, or on the side of duplicating someone, I encourage you to take action. As Anthony Robin says: *"Don't take action. Take massive action."*

ACTION

It's the follow-through that takes massive action. And if you take massive action you can also duplicate, or be a duplicator. Many companies or organizations follow the "Big Brother" theory where, *"Someone's been there before, someone's done it before, so listen, believe, and follow."* If you have a mentor and you listen to what he says, and then you believe in him and you believe what he does, then you've got to follow-through.

I'll give you an example. Just a few weeks ago I asked my main recruiter to meet me at the office at 6:30am. So he was listening but I don't think he really believed me very much because he says, "What's the point of being there at 6:30? The phone's not going to ring anyways." And then follow-through? He wasn't there. However, I had a new person who *was* there when I got to the office, and therefore, she was listening. She was believing and she was following through. Later in the day, I explained to the guy what we got done between 6:30am and 8:00am and he was like, "Oh wow. I should have been here."

• • •

In the lower part of your ladder, you're not there yet, you haven't climbed the ladder yet. You're not supposed to have the answers, you're not supposed to know everything. So learn to listen, believe, and follow your mentor(s) because they've been there; they have the answers and they have the solution.

6

PURPOSE

STEP **N**UMBER **S**IX on the ladder of success—and I believe one of the greatest keys to success—is *Purpose.* We were put on this earth to do much more than just be achievers and part of our purpose is to impact others, to impact Nations.

One thing I've realized since I got into my business—after things were rolling and the money was coming in—was that I had much more purpose than just to be successful in the marketplace. It's when you realize there is something bigger beyond your success, something greater than your success in business ... that there's another dimension beyond that.

CREATING A VISION

When my wife and I were newlyweds, I had a vision. I was on an airplane when I received the vision, and I have found many times throughout my life the Lord speaks to me when I'm in the air, maybe because I'm closer to Him. I was flying back from an international trip, and I had a vision of Costa Rica. Maybe it was partially because my wife is half-Costa Rican but I believe that it is all part of the purpose that God intended for her life before she was born, and before I was born or before we were brought together in marriage. We had talked about how we wanted to make an impact in the world, how we wanted to make a difference in Costa Rica.

I saw a children's camp in Costa Rica in the vision, and then the Lord just let me draw it out. I saw myself sitting there in a relaxed atmosphere and I started thinking outside the box. I believe purpose and thinking outside the box go hand in hand. It was a camp of restoration; a camp where fathers and sons, mothers and daughters and families could come and be reunited. As it became clearer, I saw a vision of a father-son combo or mother-daughter combo. Not so much a drug rehab but more like a *reunited rehab* or reunited center. I saw everything there from a chapel where we would have praise and worship and various guest speakers as well as cabins, hiking, and white-water rafting. It could be a session of one week or a two-week session or a three-day journey.

Not only would it be a beautiful vacation destination, it would also be the heartbeat of a restoration ministry. The idea would be for "father hasn't spoken to his son for seven years" then they could meet there and through the power of prayer, the power of God, and the power of time spent together, restore their relationship. Ideally it would be an international camp and people would come from all over the world. It would be a high-end, high quality camp. The idea would be for us to purchase some property in the near future, and then really just let the vision unfold itself, everything from a chapel to a set of cabins, maybe even a hotel like in a resort.

I believe that the purpose of everyone's life is a

combination of all their minutes, hours, days, weeks, and years on this planet. Being away from my father for four years early in my career may have been something that drove my vision. But really there was something more to it than that. I love children, I love people, and I believe that this would be a unique project. I don't know of anywhere in the world like this. It would be similar to a summer camp for kids, but maybe more for families and the mission would be "relationship restoration."

When you have made a shift in your consciousness and you're thinking in this manner, becoming top in your industry or becoming number one is a complete by-product of your purpose. This is about much more than motivation, I call this "inspiration" or living *in-spirit*. When you're inspired to change the world and to make a difference, then your business becomes simple, it becomes easy and the ladder looks a lot less steep. When you have a purpose, you have a sense of urgency—*purpose propels inspiration*. It allows you to move up because it's about more than just the self.

Another revelation of purpose came when my wife and I were in church. There was a video where our previous pastor was sharing her vision for the children and orphans in Seattle. That church in Kirkland, Washington, had built 22 homes adjacent to the church and it's primarily foster families that live there. My wife and I looked at each other and we both had a tear coming down our eye. Even in our county—in our own back yard—there was an opportunity to become foster parents and we knew that we needed to get involved.

We both had a heart for children and we both really sensed in our spirit that we were meant to be foster parents. My wife is from a family of four. Her parents have been married for 47 years and it's just her and her brother. I'm one of four children and my parents were divorced. My dad remarried to a woman with three children, and then they adopted nine children, making me one of 16 children.

TAKING ACTION

Part of our purpose is *taking action,* so we looked into it. We didn't wait around and immediately got busy on it and within 10 months we became foster parents. We currently live in Cottages, which is the community of 22 foster homes, but at the time we weren't living there and had to begin the process of relocating. We felt it was a good plan to live in the community and it's been a blessing to have people that are of the "same vision, same dream" as you. We've been responsible as respite and foster care. We will get a child placed in our home for 24 to 48 hours—it's usually a transitional period—and we've cared for about 25 different children, some of the children four to seven different times.

This has been a life changing moment where we can be successful at the office and also have an impact on a young child's life. I believe this is just the start to the purpose of our destiny, the purpose of our journey. As you can see here as we're climbing the ladder of success, it's not just about burning desire or knowing your product and it's not just about those intense moments. Yes, those are important. But once you can master those—once you can get the positive attitude down—I believe at this point we can be used for a purpose. We can be used and designed to make a difference.

Recently I had the privilege of traveling with one of my spiritual fathers. We went to a particular nation where there were over 2,000 missionaries there. We were able to sow into this mission because our business has been healthy, our business has been prospering, and we made some wise decisions. We were able to sow not only monetary, but we were able to sow our time. My wife was home, she was my cheerleader, my encourager. I went there and we spoke to leaders—over 800 different leaders at one time—in a five-day period. Why would I do this? Because the purpose is much bigger than just rising the ladder of success of what we've been called to do in our marketplace. It's a great satisfaction in purpose.

To have a successful marriage, that might be the purpose. Or you may have a book inside you or you may have a conference inside you that the world needs to hear. When you can get the concept of purpose, anything is possible. In addition to this, life is much bigger than money. Yes, I believe money is important, but what's more important are the people in your community and the people across the globe.

You know one thing that we've done in our purpose is we also have been big givers. What do we give? We give some money and we give some time but most importantly, we give the gift that God has given us to go to new levels, to go to new heights. I love speaking to people, I love increasing people and I love the ability to think outside the box. Because of the purpose in my life, because of the purpose of my wife's life and the purpose that we've been called to do, we can change people's lives, we can change cities, and we change nations.

When you are a purpose-driven man or woman, you're not only affecting your family, but you're affecting everyone you come in contact with. It could be a smile at the airport, it could be a handshake in the hallway, or saying hello to someone in the elevator. I believe that as you are purpose driven, you also become an *encourager*. As I've been encouraged my entire career it's now time for me to give back and encourage people. Once again, the purpose could be something small, it could be something medium or could be something big, but when you find your purpose, I believe the sky's the limit.

ANOTHER LADDER

What this has done for me? It has created *many new ladders.* The ladder of success is great and now there's a new desire that's brewing in my spirit and in my heart. A ladder for the people that come in my office, a ladder for my community, a ladder for the children, and a ladder for the world. I believe that God will give us more than one ladder.

When there's a purpose in your life, all these ladders

will appear and fall into place. As you increase your thinking, as you increase who are becoming, more ladders will appear in your life. And each of these ladders can serve as your purpose because I believe that each of us can be a man or woman of many purposes. And your purpose, or purposes, will effect not only your children but your children's children and your neighbor's children. I just want to encourage you, as you find your purpose the doors will be open and the ladders will appear. And then there will be new ladders, there will be new opportunities.

Your ladders can serve many purposes, and many successes. One ladder could be your business, another ladder could be in your marriage, another one your family. Another one might be in your higher calling or your purpose; as in my case, the Costa Rican camp or fostering nearby children. Every single area of your life is a ladder; your business, finances, health, marriage, being a father, being a leader to the people that are underneath you, being involved in the ministry.

I believe that success really is about being well-rounded. You have to be successful in all areas in your life. Of course, one might have more of a prayer in this season or that season but overall, every single area of your life is a ladder, and every single area of your life is a challenge based off the spirit of excellence.

Finding the purpose—it's the key, that's the secret. It will help rise you to the top and I want you to know it is possible. I'm telling you—from where I came to where I'm am now—*if I can do it, you can do it.* I'm here to encourage you and I'm here to tell you that it is possible.

It becomes challenging as you continue to grow, I know. I'm involved heavily in my ministry and if I was to stay the same today that I was two years ago, then I wouldn't have any growth. Part of success is understanding personal growth along with personal development will help you to grow forward and climb higher.

• • •

Each of you are a winner and each of you have a purpose. Sometimes it just takes saying it over and over again to get things moving. Positive affirmations are the motivating force behind getting inspired, getting "in-spirit," and helps remind you that God has a purpose for you and a plan for you. You can do it. You will do it. Just keep saying it. When you say it long enough then it becomes a belief. Then when you believe something, anything is possible. If you can see it and you can believe it, your purpose can be fulfilled.

———~~~———

7

THE POWER OF GOD AND PRAYER

S TEP **NUMBER SEVEN** on the ladder of success is *the power of God and prayer.* I've had the honor and privilege of being in a good church, being around inspirational people and men of God my whole adult life. The power of God is absolutely amazing and I believe one of the keys to my success is being sensitive to His voice. I've learned this over the years through practice, drill and rehearsal. I've studied men of God,

I've been in church and I've attended seminars—I've had to work hard and learn to be still and listen.

Success is not something I was born with, it's not something that you're born with. Success is something you grow into and something that you are led to, as in *"You have to lead them to success."* Success is a by-product of hard work, personal growth, spiritual growth and maturation.

In the beginning there's a huge learning curve in so many areas. Allow yourself to be coachable. And on the spiritual side, just believe what the Word of God says. Learn to be sensitive to His voice. I believe this is one of the keys to climbing the ladder which is even beyond purpose—*our Divine Anointing awaits us.* The Anointing—it is so sweet and so powerful.

BE STILL, BE SILENT

Here is a story that you may be able to relate to. As I mentioned in the beginning of Chapter 3, I was at a crossroads in my career and felt like I needed to move two states away to move forward. I would be leaving a business that was bringing in $100,000 a month and start over. It was not an easy thing for me to do but I found myself packing everything in my car. The inner voice was so strong that it was undeniable, I needed to go. But it was possible because I had peace, I had the peace of God. When it feels right, it's just right. I believe it is important that when God speaks to you that you take action. These things allowed me to be able to move forward in faith.

I knew I had to take a risk, I had to be bold. But I also knew when I got there that something good was going to take place. I met my wife just a few months later and we now have three beautiful children. It's amazing when you follow that voice, when you follow your gut feeling, what's possible. At the time relocating was outside the box but I had to move, I had to separate myself, I had to take a chance. This is the power of God.

Seek counsel from your mentor at all times, but at the end of the day God's wisdom is more powerful than any man's counsel. Wisdom is more precious than counsel so I think it's important to seek wisdom. I put myself in good places and various venues, I attended morning breakfasts, workshops and prayer chains— these are all things that help. We've been blessed in so many ways. We've had the honor and privilege of connecting with so many people around the globe. I have my wife's mother praying for me. I've got various friends in my church praying for me. I have various prophets around the world praying for me.

Being planted in the Word of God is absolutely important as you grow and prosper. The benefit of that is the seeds will then grow and sprout into the fruits of the Spirit of joy, patience and peace. The opposite of this will be anger, unhappiness, rage, and so on. *Anger is one letter short of danger.* How can there be success in your life if you are living a life of anger and danger?

I believe prayer is important, in my daily walk and in my business. I will sometimes shoot "arrow prayers" at work like, *"Lord give me some grace. How do I handle this?"* I think arrow prayers are important for a business man or business woman as they're going through a busy day. It doesn't mean that you have to be in your closet on your knees praying, you can be praying while you're driving; you can be praying at your desk, on the airplane, or in a business meeting.

I believe this goes back to the basic principles, the first six steps of the ladder and the "law of attraction." I got placed in a church that prays from 10pm to 1am—we pray for nations, we pray for businesses. As my business has grown, my destiny has shifted. It's important that your thoughts go to your words and your words go to your actions, your actions go to your habits and your habits go to your character. And the best of all after your character is your destiny.

Prayer moves things; prayer shift things. The verse that comes to my mind is Matthew 6:33: *Seek first the Kingdom of God and all the things will be added unto you.* I've probably focused on that verse more than any other verse on this journey. As you seek God first, all these things will be added unto you. Almost every decision that I make, I think of that verse. *What do you seek, what things are you looking for?*

THE POWER OF THE MUSTARD SEED

I think props are important too. Like in the Bible it says, *"If you have faith the size of a mustard seed, you can say to this mountain 'Move' and it shall be moved (Matthew 17:20)."* I don't think God is talking about Mount Rainier or Mount Shasta, or any mountain around the world. He's talking about the mountain in your life. So for the longest time ever, I had a jar of mustard seeds in my car as a reminder of my faith. So if you're facing a mountain, just look at the mustard seed then you can revert back to the Word of God. That prop, something as small as a mustard seed, helps center you and get you back on the correct way of thinking.

You can only go so far on man's advice—you can go a lot further on God' wisdom. And you don't have to be a Christian to benefit from that truth. God rewards the principles, not necessarily the person. And the principles are the same all over the world. One of the wealthiest men in the world is Bill Gates, but he's also one of the most generous givers there is and strives to reduce the inequity in the world. Gravity works for all mankind and it operates as a law, the Law of Giving.

Another favorite verse of mine is Romans 8:14: *For those who are led by the Spirit of God are the children of God.* We are *led* by the Spirit of God, we are not dragged, forced, or imposed upon. The direction I take my team at work, we're led by the Spirit. Everything we do from the car we drive and the trips we take, we're led by the Spirit.

Ultimately I believe it is about more than purpose alone because now we're talking about destiny. We're talking about my children and my children's children. This is the power of prayer. This is the power of knowing that there's much more out there than just being successful in the marketplace. Whether it's being a foster parent or we're out there to change the nation, I believe that all this is a product of prayer.

And it is also a product of environment. One thing I've learned in my business is that atmosphere is everything. Yes, we can control the atmospheres we are in; we can choose to stay or we can choose to leave. I encourage you to be mindful of those around you and about the atmosphere you're in and choose the right atmosphere.

> You may be on the right ladder
> but in the wrong atmosphere.

Be still and pay attention to your surroundings. You may need to switch your ladder, you may need to get into a new atmosphere. As your atmosphere grows, as your tent pegs grow, you're going to see yourself go to new heights, to new levels that you never knew were possible.

A LIFE VERSE

One of my great friends, he was the voice of *"Flounder"* in the famous movie "The Little Mermaid"—he always calls me "the elevator." I believe this is an important quality because as I can elevate myself, I can also elevate people around me. How do we do this? By encouraging them, by finding the best in them. Many times I don't even tell them that we're praying for them.

So, in your business I encourage you to pray. I can't tell you how many times my wife prayed for the right recruiter. In your life I encourage you to do strategic prayers. But not only are we praying for the right person, but the right time. You can read and study the best book which is the Bible. I believe in the universal principle of the Bible, I believe in the power of *the Bible as a Handbook for Success.* It's better than all the books written together and it helps me in every area of life, whether it's my call for Costa Rica, being a father or being a business man. If you use that to build your life, if you just do that to have principles, you'll see your career go to new heights—you'll see new and different levels, meet new people and make new friends. All these things will be added unto you because we're seeking Him first. It's a life verse.

We all need a life verse—we all need a life quote. We all need a mission statement for our family; we all need to have a plan and a purpose. This all goes back to clarity, which I was mentioning earlier. When you're clear on something, anything is possible. When you know where you're going the sky's the limit.

I encourage you find a good church, find a good mentor, and find a good coach. Behind every good man is a great woman. I could never do all this without my wife. I'm so thankful for my wife and I let her know that I'm thankful. Do you let your wife know you're thankful for her? Are you telling your children that you love them? My father taught me love.

I believe love is the greatest asset to this whole package. God is love. *For God so loved the world that He gave His only begotten son (John 3:16).* If you can just go out there and understand the principles of God, I'm telling you anything is possible. Your world will be shifted, your world will be changed. Then *you* can become a world change; a world shifter. I believe God has the best for you. I believe, that you haven't seen nothing yet.

"But as it is written, Eye hath not seen, nor ear heard, neither have entered into the heart of man, the things which God hath prepared for them that love him."
—1 Corinthians 2:9

As we put these principles in the place, as we move forward, as we have a burning desire—anything is possible. Yes, it takes work … it takes sacrifice … it takes effort. And yes, you have to take risk. But understand that there's a purpose for you and then you can duplicate it. It's not just about Josh being successful or the Liskes being successful. This is about everyone that hears this or read this. It's about you being successful; knowing that you can do it.

Many people operate out of fear. I operate out of optimism. You've got to be optimistic. You've got to take action. You've got take a risk. As you go, God will open doors. As you move forward, a new ladder will appear. Be strong. Find a good church. Seek a man of God to speak into your life, then you can be the encourager. We must be encouraged first before we'll become the encourager.

As you are putting God first and you are knowing exactly through Him, He's going to give you ideas and He's going to give you direction for life. As we are praying, as we're seeking Him, as we're knocking—*He will answer.* He will open the door and He will open a door that no man can open and He will close a door that no man can shut.

As you start succeeding and having success, as you start having a movement and your ladder starts growing, be mindful of duplication because along the journey, your success will become a magnet. You'll see yourself being successful and then all of sudden two, three, or four other people will arrive and as these doors open you'll see a new journey, a new ladder, a new success. This is the power of duplication.

It's no good if just you rise to the occasion. It's no good if you're just a gold medalist—there are other people that want that goal, that deserve the gold, so share the bounty of your blessings. It's great to be number one, but the greatest feeling that I've probably felt my entire career is seeing that young seventeen-year-old boy rise, and see his smile and the twinkle in his eye, and see his life transformed because of prayer and because of the power of duplication.

This is what it all comes down to is that when you have a purpose, when you have a calling. You'll be motivated to move mountains but much more than motivation, you'll be *inspired.* You'll be inspired—working *in-spirit*—to do things that you never imagined. And as you go; I encourage you to walk the walk; not only talk the talk, but walk in faith that you're going to be bold like a lion. I encourage you to be bold, to go and be strong. Get a book, get a tape, surround yourself with winners. It will take a positive attitude. You might have to separate yourself from friends, maybe even the close ones, for a while. You'll need to get your spouse behind you, they're your greatest cheerleader, as well as some in your immediate family because they're there to encourage you, to empower you.

You *will* have some intense moments so don't get discouraged and remind yourself that *there's a reason for a season of intensity.* Every champion spent time in the gym, every Olympic medalist makes a sacrifice. You may have blown out a knee—get back on the treadmill. You may have had a bankrupt business—start a new business. Get intense.

You will need to be intentional for a season, but understand that this is the focus, the laser beam focus we were talking about earlier. Product knowledge becomes easy as we're focused, as we have a good attitude, as we understand our purpose with prayers behind us. How can you not have a burning desire when there's prayer behind you?

How can you not be excited about life—*how can you not be excited about your dreams?* I encourage you to chase your dreams, go after your dreams and the burning desire will become much greater. As God gives you new ladders your desire will change. When I first started my career, I didn't think about my mission of serving other nations, I didn't think about being a world changer or a public speaker. But I can tell you:

> When you do things right—
> what starts right ends right.

• • •

I hope your journey is as great as mine. Go. Be strong. Be blessed. And let me pray:

Dear Lord, I thank you for every person that reads this and hears my message. Let them go and be prosperous. Give them creative ideas. Take them to new heights. Show them things that only You can do. I pray for miracles. I pray for signs. I pray for wonders. Lord, if you can do it for me; do it for them. And I thank you Lord for what I got from your great spirit. Move these people; change their hearts. Let families be restored. Let businesses be healed because of the mighty power of this prayer in God's name. Amen.

CPSIA information can be obtained at www.ICGtesting.com
Printed in the USA
BVOW05s2332260216

438274BV00004B/8/P